GOVERNOR'S CLUB

My Time Behind The Bar

By John DeRosa

authorHOUSE®

AuthorHouse™
1663 Liberty Drive
Bloomington, IN 47403
www.authorhouse.com
Phone: 1 (800) 839-8640

Published by AuthorHouse 01/26/2018

ISBN: 978-1-5462-2475-4 (sc)
ISBN: 978-1-5462-2474-7 (e)

Library of Congress Control Number: 2018900690

Print information available on the last page.

Any people depicted in stock imagery provided by Thinkstock are models, and such images are being used for illustrative purposes only. Certain stock imagery © Thinkstock.

This book is printed on acid-free paper.

Because of the dynamic nature of the Internet, any web addresses or links contained in this book may have changed since publication and may no longer be valid. The views expressed in this work are solely those of the author and do not necessarily reflect the views of the publisher, and the publisher hereby disclaims any responsibility for them.

Introduction

It's mid November, 2010 I am sitting next to my campfire beneath a South Carolina evening sky in the Congaree National Park. I can see the crescent moon just beyond the nearest palm tree. In the quiet of the night my phone rings. It's my friend Amy asking how my cross country road trip to all 48 State Capitols in the continental United States of America was going. She also wanted to know when I would be returning home to Saint Petersburg Beach there was a job opportunity for me come the second week of December. She gave me the number to call Jan Boccuti, the owner of the Pasadena Bar and Grill. I informed Amy that I had two capitols left to visit and would be home for Thanksgiving. I called Jan the next day after breaking camp and agreed to meet with her upon my return. I have been on the road for three months at this point and contemplating what I was going to do for employment once my travels would come to an end.

I pull up to Pasadena Bar and Grill to meet Jan for the first time. She's looking for a bartender to replace Matt her longtime employee in about two weeks. Nervous, I stagger through the front entrance to a few hellos from some of the locals that I already knew from previous jobs. Jan walks up to me and says "wow you're pretty popular you got the job". I didn't know everyone at first so one by one I hope I gained their trust. My mother taught me that every day was an opportunity to turn a stranger into a friend. In my seven years bartending here I have been blessed with great friendships. I have laughed and cried, cheered and booed, poured heavy and at times served only water to quench the thirst we all crave in our hearts. I now thirst for another journey within my heart. March 11th, 2018 I embark upon a 2,090 mile hike across the Appalachian Trail. I must be crazy to give up this fantastic job working for a wonderful woman who cares so much about this amazing bar. I must be crazy to give up my beachfront apartment I have been blessed to call my personal paradise for the last fifteen years. I must be out of my mind to traverse the forest when i have found trust, companionship, and inspiration in the eyes and heart of a beautiful girlfriend. I am the happiest now than I have been my entire life. I must be crazy to put all of this on hold to go get lost in nature.

With this book of poetry and inspiration written every other Sunday for seven years i want to share with the world the Kindest and Loving People I have ever met. Now I know why my mother bartended all those years. She loved the people. If you ever get a chance to stop by the Pasadena Bar and Grill to wet your whistle or get the best burger in town, tell them Johnny Says Hello.

Vern and Buzz

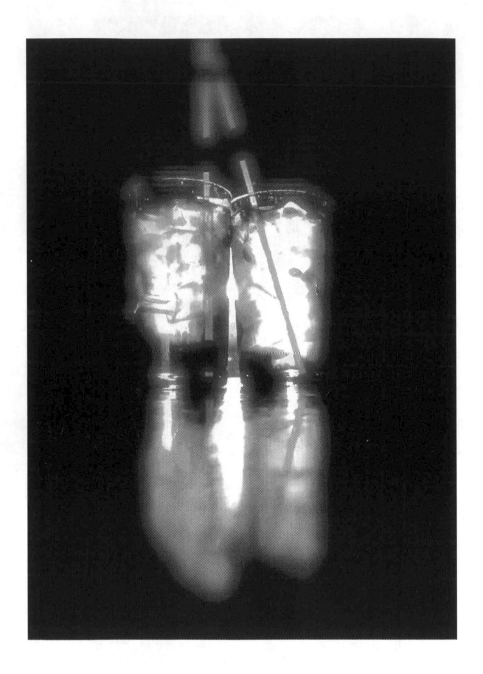

AMIDST THE SMOKE AND ECHOES
OF HARD TIMES IN A
WORLD FULL OF COLOR,
I HEAR GREAT CONVERSATION OF
KINDNESS AND HAPPINESS
WITHIN THESE FOUR WALLS.

PASADENA
BAR & GRILL

Amidst the smoke
and echos of hard
times in a world
full of color
I hear great
conversation of kindness
and happiness within
these four walls

Johnny

A SLAVE TO SILENCE
LOST IN A FAR AWAY ECHO
FOUND IN AN ENCLOSURE
FULL OF FRIENDS
AND EMPTY BOTTLES
THE NIGHT NOW DAY
AS I TURN OUT
THE LAST LIGHT
I RETURN TO WHERE
DREAMS ARE NEVER FORGOTTEN

SIMPLE PLEASURES of
YESTERDAY Tomorrows
    Treasures FOR SALE
Repititious Memories
    Day Dreams FADED Years
Sitting next to neon signs
    sending me your way
Lost in a near forgotten Smile
    I hope to touch again
So take me back   to
    simple pleasures
Release Me To Blue Skies
    And FADED DREAMS

Remnants of conversation
  The echo of lost WINDS
Back in the day
  The humor of / good friends
You get to know yourself
  Through the people you meet
Musical chairs
  Last one to find their seat
Conspiracy of Good Times
  Had all day long
Dancing under blue stars
  Last Call — One More Song

NEON REFLECTIONS
 Sunset Collections
Bottled Nectars shine
   JUICE OF THY VINE
Groves within the WIND
   Emotions that blend
Concoction of the past
   Slowly to the glass
Dances upon her lips
   A gentle smile slips
 Make-Out sessions
 UNDER NEON Reflections

Morning sun and beginning
of shadows
First to rise from slumbering dreams

Ease into the day
like blossoming flowers

Passion to be perfect
a journey of extremes
Seperated by reality
destination of trends

Chasing the days
of lost conversation
Gathering laughter
and echo of friends

Evening sun melts into
tomorrow's fascination

Inspire
To Be
yourself

Change of season
changing one's mind
Change for no reason
loose change you may find
Lost is forever
if you give up the search
Finding peace in a sunset
the horizon holds church
Love in masses
sharing warmth from the heart
Captured is kindness
ignored from the start
Change of scenery
changing one's view
Change for a good reason
the change all up to you

Time comes and goes
like slow rain and tears
Swimming with echoes
journey of years
Orbiting in spirit
an uphill stream
Floating beneath
an endless dream
Taking from life all
that is left
Drowning in sunsets
that steal your breath
Story of color
all horizons supply
Looking beyond
an ageless sky

Johnny

Born to a new day
   Awaken to fresh ideas
Reach for the sky
   To see how it feels
Walking on clouds
      My soles changing views
Stepping out of a shadow
   Reflections of torched hues
The distance between
      now and yesterday
Is a lost memory
   we find along the way
Facing a line-up of bottles
   nectars beyond the horizon
Sitting next to faces
   I wait to see again

Johnny

EMERGE INTO EXISTENCE
Like the sun shining on a new day
SPEAK TO ME SKY OF WONDER
early riser Nature's bouquet
Display for me hope in a
quiet voice that sings a song
Living in harmony beneath the clouds
where dreams belong
Walk with me until I fly
above all I have learned
Freefalling with tomorrow's sun
do not be concerned

DREAM - CREATE - EXPLORE
Shawn

Governor's Club Exclusive

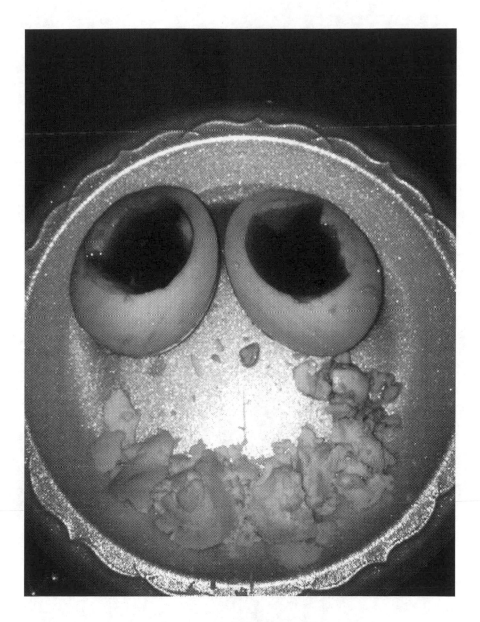

Infamous Birthday Egger Shot

Closing Time

Harbor Light Night

Rise with as when life
shines through your window
Walk toward me when
slowly opens your heart
Close your eyes once you
become absent minded
Steep in your thoughts
lies the next journey
Sunsets melt into tomorrow's
never ending wake

Share with others a smile
when you find it hard to cry
Inside your wandering soul
is a fresh attempt
to feel the love
KINDNESS IS FREE

Asleep to new ideas
   Freedom on the run
Receptions of nature
   your face's slapped by the sun
Palm trees blow in the wind
   like a bad hair day
Reflections of tomorrow
   our memories of yesterday
Get lost in the horizon
   blind every now and then
Unpure thoughts awake
   your mirrored opinion
Leaves an impression
   in dreams under the moon
Falling into place   our melting
   youth settles soon

Go out and create life
instead of watching it create you
Paradise in the distance transparent
beyond the horizons view
In between the pages
of nature's thunderous joys
Chase you inside
sky of grey and noise
Pleasures your anguish
cold tears from above
Stern against the storm
estranged winds provide the shove
Drowning in solitude
the warmth of good friends
Neon reflections remind us
of yesterday's trends

We remember nothing...
afraid of our first light
Hard times on the rocks
easy on the ice
Crawl into the darkness
dirty knees the next day
Far away echoes...
last apologies along the way
Some weigh their dreams
depth of an empty start
Ignoring the stranger who
sits next to a lonely heart
Excuse me tomorrow
for how I once felt
I LOVE these four walls
that allow me to melt

Moon shines thru the dreams
of a mountain man
Liquid perception
bold colors of the land
Burning the weed
our freedoms in harvest grows
Buried seeds of promise
acres in perfect rows
Imprisoned spirits a line-up
of labels and grain
Inspiration beneath courage
waiting for rain
Senses of nature
sees nothing hears everything
Pour shots for my friends
life continues to sing

24

The wind is your breath
the sky your eyes
The spirit within never leaves never dies
Your soul in flight
now feels the sunrise as the sun sets
Off to the land of grace
free falling in faith no nets
We will catch you in memory David
and smile through our tears
Celebrate your life as we
continue through the years
You gave us joy in repetition
laughter with no end
We give you our reflection of love
to continue your journey/our friend
The wind is your breath
the sky/your eyes
The spirit within
never leaves never dies

6/24/12 — MUCH LOVE — Schan

25

Chase me into the light
    inescapable dreams
Awaken to a sound further
    than far away seems
Echoes in thought
    charades in the wind
Dancing grandiloquently
    time and time again
Catch me catching my breath
    this horizon I follow
Approaching the death of today
    the birth of tomorrow
Melting in unison the deepest sky
    the darkest sea
Asleep in faith the setting sun
    that sets me free

7/8/13

Take me inside
to see the landscape of thought
Out of mind expressions
the spirits have bought
Daydreams in a bottle
captures the escape of time
Reflection of a shadow
a memory at its prime
Release me outside
to hear society scream
Out of body experience
away from the dream
Beyond a crowd of strangers
a falling star shines
In the darkest of days
good friends here are
common to find

In the darkest of days
good friends here
are common to find
Beyond a crowd of strangers
a falling star shines
Out of body experience
away from the dream
Release me outside
to hear society scream
Reflection of a shadow
a memory at its prime
Daydreams in a bottle
captures the escape of time
Out of mind expressions
the spirits have bought
Take me inside
to see the landscape
of thought

Journey within a dream
Is it further than it seems
Take me to a beautiful day
In a memory where I want to stay
Wake me up if I fall asleep
To another promise I fail to keep

Burry me with a shovel
I have died before
Escaping to a freedom
that allows me to explore
Release me to nature
that captures my soul
Happiness is a journey
this is my role

The Sun Is Over The Yardarm

Squire Humor

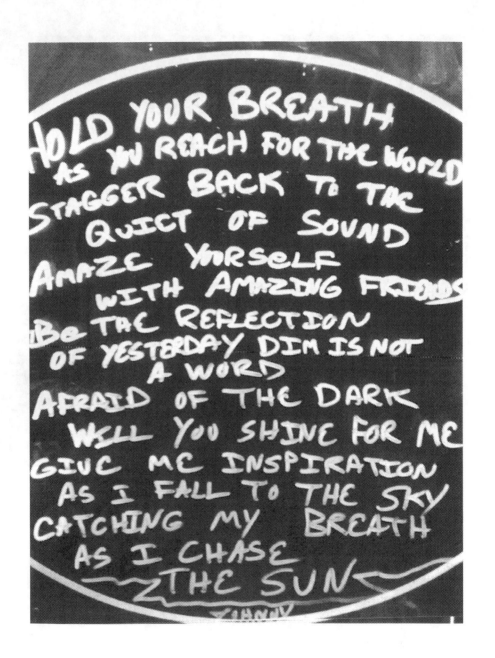

I can smile knowing you
are here without being here
Taken far away from now
ten seconds ahead
Elapsed thoughts forgotten
in another kiss from yesterday
Tastes differently with
fresh memories of you
Older than a conversation
lost in the wind
I find myself dancing
with your shadow

10/1/12

How far is it
    to far enough
A sunset in the battle
    of a forgotten day
Brighter than a memory
    that has lost it's way
Further than we
    dare to roam
Too close for comfort
    yet closer to home
We travel down dusty roads
    blind from the start
Away from the beauty
    that waits in one's heart
We can't be found without
    getting lost

I walk quietly in a
    forest of many
One flower beneath the
    tallest of trees
Beyond the shadows
    of tomorrows setting sun
A cloud out of character
    looks like min
Freedom of my spirit
    a harvest of jrys
Replinishes the hope
    in yesterdays dreams
I enjoy this view of
life with all my friend

10/29/12

Take from life all hope
that drowns in the mirror
Opening your heart
to something more clearer
Share with all the kindness
that flows free with the winds
Stretching across the horizon
that soulfully mends
Guide us through our
daydreams before we go blind
Impressions in the sky are
treasured friendships
We find

1/28/13   Johnny

Iron the wrinkles of my
loathing heart's pulse
Sign of no father no son
no bridges to cross
I travel where no one
has sent me before
Release myself to brighter
days to explore
Beyond an over poured glass
and a goodnight kiss
I wonder if the rest of the
world knows I exist
Home away from home not as
far as it may seem
Quietly my heart returns
to a place I freely dream

Lost in reality the path
of forgotten skies
Reflection of a kind thought
the sunset in disguise
Fray of day and night
tipping of the scales
Appreciating the hidden balance
mother nature unvails
Pulse of a sonorous imagination
the horizon's pride
Watching life's joy within
erupt tide after tide

1/3/13 Johnny

My words
are echoes of your actions
Disregard the thoughts
of uninterrupted value...
A lost wind refreshes
our tone of acceptance
Perception of something missing
within ourselves
We find out we are
the cool breeze on a sad day
Smoke signals from afar
softly drift toward us
May our peace of mind
escape the abundance of hate

If I was a song
I would dance with
all my friends

Shawn 3/12/13

41

Ease into the grey
of a new beginning
Dark of the day becomes
the light of the night
Our trust put to the limit
of no end

We are conscience over
matter we go it alone
Follow the mood as we
fade into last call
A dream outside the fog
of one more smoke
Find ourselves staggering
for love
Curtains are drawn
It is only sleep that awaits

DREAM MY FRIENDS

3/25/13

Tomorrow further than
far away seems
Kind thoughts heal the
souls of broken dreams
How many times do we
fail to share
Discovery of choices
who to help if we dare
Perception of happiness
a smile on display
Honesty matters no matter
how far one strays
Only we can be true to
ourselves....

4/9/15

43

Shift Change

Drinking Problem

One Too Many

Happy Hour Nap Time

Find myself pacing
as my mind runs away
Fulfilling an empty heart
refilling another glass
Lost in an abyss
of smoke and last
breath's
Replenishing a lost
smile that lives
in yesterday
7/24/13 Johnny

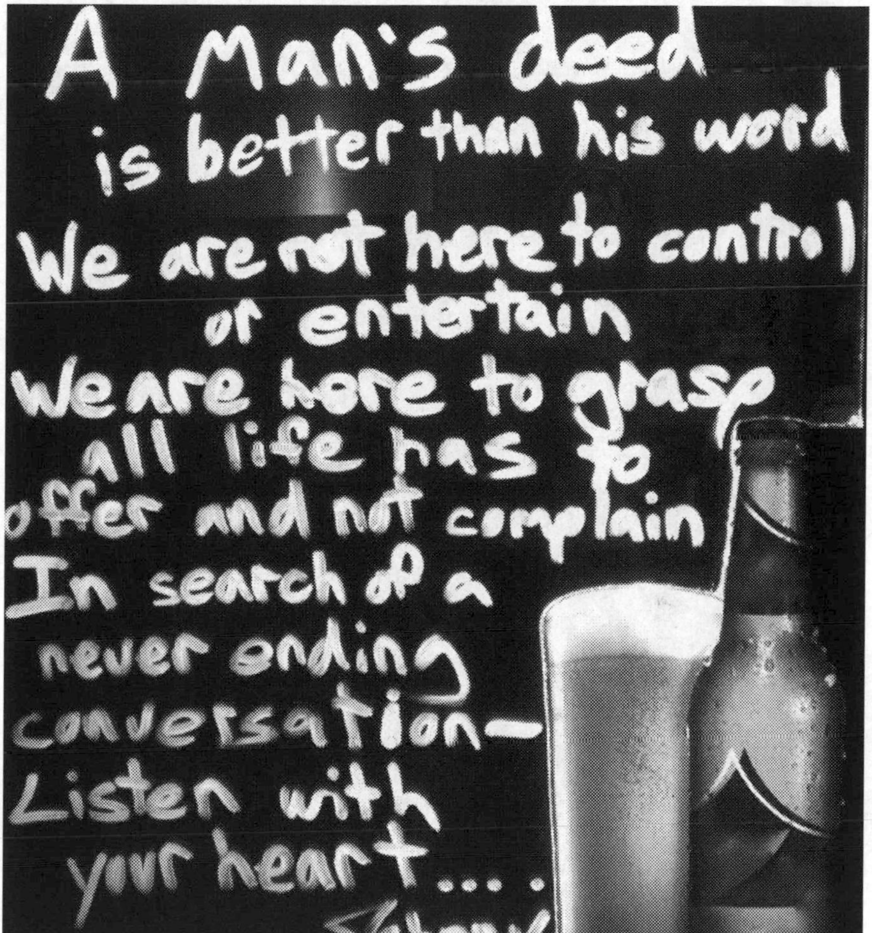
A Man's deed
is better than his word
We are not here to control
or entertain
We are here to grasp
all life has to
offer and not complain
In search of a
never ending
conversation—
Listen with
your heart....

Give me a shade beneath
the sun
A place to dream amidst
the fun
Shadows protect those afraid
to roam
Give me paradise A place
to call home
I fall as I stumble
through the clouds

And find myself
thinking
ALOUD......
7/22/13   Johnny

50

Happiness is a gift
the message it sends
Our family of strangers
should all be best friends
Abandoned too often
the opportunity to shine
Break out of your
prison created
in mind

—Johnny—
10/7/13

51

Echoes of yesterday
  whisper in silence
Fray of day and night
  the sun melts without violence
In search of happiness
  a sky full of blue
Chasing a memory
  enjoying the view
Strong shot of courage
  money well spent
Come on in
    We have
Barstools for rent
11/11/13 Johnny

Clear me a path
    of smoke and tongue
Speaking to shadows
    are the old and young
Whisper me a sonnet
    that has six lines
Drink with me a nectar
    that has no vines
Chase away the echoes
    that run away first
And reward me
    with an eternal
Thirst —Johan
    1/6/14

While you are pondering
    my brush to canvas
Know that the wind paints
    the way we feel
Tell me a story
    layered with decades
A collection of thoughts
    that gracefully mends
Stare at life's medium
    with eyes wide open
And enjoy breathless
    etchings of time
    upon sand......
1/26/14   Johnny

Listen quietly for the spirit of living
I will lend you a piece of my heart
The noises from life are our echoes in silence
Far away memories that roll down our cheeks
Whisper softly to me the joys of giving
I will offer you all that I am
Sometimes the greatest of all gifts
Is a gentle smile from
a complete stranger
How strange it is
to see a bar
full of
Smiles ☺

2/9/14 Johnny

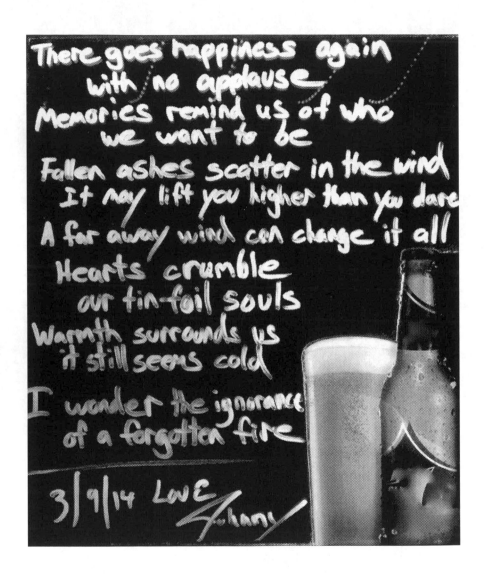

There goes happiness again
with no applause
Memories remind us of who
we want to be
Fallen ashes scatter in the wind
It may lift you higher than you dare
A far away wind can change it all
Hearts crumble
our tin-foil souls
Warmth surrounds us
it still seems cold
I wonder the ignorance
of a forgotten fire

3/9/14 LOVE Johnny

$ 25⁰⁰ BAR TAB

TO WHO EVER
POKES (BOH)
—ANDY—
THE MOST

2/17-2/22 Johnny

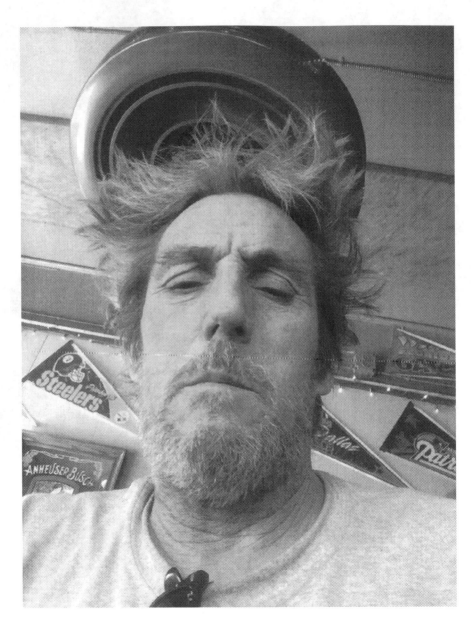

Ball of Hate

Tumbleweed

Last Glass of Sobriety

The Man - The Myth - The Legend

A TUMBLEWEED is the above ground part of any number of things that once mature and dry, disengage from their root and tumble away in the wind. The TUMBLEWEED is a diaspore aiding in dispersal of propagules as it tumbles, or after it has come to rest in a wet location —¶CD—

No more shots for TUMBLEWEED

Nothing But Pokes

If tomorrow brings rain
and alters my view
I will wander beneath yesterday's
sky I choose
The horizon portrays
a collision of blues
Melting is the day, a sunset
with peaceful hues
Expressions from a whisper
a conversation brand new
Thinking of you
a smile so true
Smile at me and
I will smile too
I never knew beautiful
was as beautiful
as you
4/22/11

It is beautiful from afar to know that
you are there and I am here
I was there once in the past a dream
never to last it was still beautiful
from a far - I see smiles
in friends when the laughter begins it is
still beautiful from afar - When we
become wise and our childhood dies
- we are still beautiful from afar
When humanity cries and peace
replies - it is still and beautiful
from afar - When the angels
fly beneath a blue sky
they are beautiful
from afar - It is
true I will always
think of you so
beautiful from afar
Johnny   4-6-14

My shadow is one dimension
the light I hide inside
Escaping happiness beneath
a blue sky that collides
The reflection of yesterday
never fades away
Curious I am how much
sun will shine today
Life is a true story
If you truly believe
Parading happiness
with every breath
that I breathe

5/5/14

Can you see my hurt
behind my happiness
It is the saddest view
beneath blue skies

When we smile
our friends smile
Ignoring the spirit
of everything living
We lose all aspects
of anything natural
We are surrounded
by beauty
We see what our hearts
allow us to feel

ERASE IGNORANCE
5/19/14   Johann

We create these places called nests — places where we can hide our thoughts — our cages — our prisons we create for ourselves — water forms to ice and melts fire into ash — I hear voices with no faces — sometimes we soar too high to see what lies ahead — Smile and free my mind — Smile and free yours — ♥CD— 6/1/14

Life has been breath taking from the very
start — Share with us the beauty
of your heart — Come sit by the
waters edge the melting horizon
is on display — Gather around and
listen to tales of yesterday — Escape
into a whisper the voice of a
dear friend — Traverse winds
hold together the pure spirits
that blend — Helpless is a
blue sky that bleeds
into the night —
Until the orbiting
fire returns at
first light — Johnny

Life is a true story / 6/15/14

68

A voice goes unnoticed if you ignore its origin — I hear footprints approaching every now and then — THE HEARTBEAT OF A FRIEND IS THE PULSE OF HAPPINESS — Lonely is a lost memory from a near forgotten kiss — We are vulnerable when we dance naked under the sun — Disrobing our beliefs laughing as we run — The wind catches up to us for we are just a gust — Scattered across a sky that only a blue horizon can trust — 7/20/14

Johnny DeRosa

Follow your reflection
    as it patiently wanders
Parallel to a horizon
    that has no shadows
Dreaming in color
    the bluest of blues
Inspiring to inspire
    a journey with no shoes
These circles
    of days
take us back
to our youth
10/22/13 Johnny

May the contrast of the twilights gleam bring joyous celebration to freedom's dream - One of the finest strangers you will ever meet - He would walk in with a smile and find himself a seat - A collector of knowledge and coins of yesterday - Humanities richest treasure was the kindness of Tom Payne - In the silence of flight that takes him higher - In the kingdom of HEAVEN he is GOD's newest SQUIRE

Heaven's Squire
- Thomas Payne -

Pasadena Love

One on the House

The PBAG

I awaken to the adolescents of darkness saying hello -

It reminds me that the quiet of life is silently left behind -

Wandering beyond the boundaries where the wild flowers grow -

I walk peacefully in dreams that escape my traversed mind -

-JCD-

We are all born with our wings -

It is up to us wether we earn our halos or our horns -

-JCD-

LIFE IS A TRUE STORY -

-JCD-

There are only two things I know for sure -

Who I am -

Who I am not -

-JCD-

if You Do Not Enjoy Life -

You Destroy Life -

-JCD-

Raindrops Are Tears of an Unknown Happiness -

-JCD-

Is the horizon 9:15 or 3:45 -

Is it day before night or night after day -

Am I more vertical to heaven or closer to hell -

-JCD-

whisper -FRAY- beautiful

The Fray lies Between a Whisper and Something Beautiful

-JCD-

Those Beneath the Rock For Which They Dwell -

Should Never Throw the First Stone -

-JCD-

Liability Rests Within the Inspiration that Motivates -

-JCD-

Do Not Drink While You Are Drinking -

-JCD-

I Have Discovered That an Act of Kindness is the Miracle -

-JCD-

Bottled up and left on the shelf -

A toast for world peace -

A drink for good health -

Liquid desire for all to see -

Crack the seal to set our spirits free -

Inner child of yesterday all grown up -

Life on the rocks drowning in a plastic cup -

-JCD-

I feel your eyes upon me when the ice melts away -

Allowing your memories to slowly replay -

Yesterday is still with us as time stays the course -

Broken hearts to broken hopes life has no remorse -

So continue to stare as I continue to shine -

Pouring you a spirit or a fresh glass of wine -

Today is upon us as tomorrow has no promises -

Raise your hearts to those we love and the anonymous -

-JCD-

Jovial sky

hOrizon on fire

deHydrated clouds lag by

dowNward falling tears

crowNed by mother nature

plentY expressions of life

adoreD by the melting sun

smilEs escape the last light

mirRored in full color

blOssoming flower of GOD

pSalms inspires thy soul

Azure heart from above

-JCD-

How does one feel all alone when the are surrounded by everyone -

Why does everyone seem so alone surrounded by emptiness-

There is a void in the middle of our lives that has no end -

The beginning of all tomorrow's start with a new rising sun -

A hope that goes unwitnessed until we extend our loving hearts -

-JCD-

There is an empty log in the corner of all tomorrows -

I sat there once yesterday expressing life's sorrows -

An anger too quiet screaming through the trees -

A voice in the forest another leaf breathes -

Change in the weather estranged is my mood -

Leaning on friends as a falling tree should -

The sky is my template the emotions I hide -

Chasing the sun my soul's eternal guide -

Missing in action the stars give me hope -

They protect me from darkness and in silence I cope -

-JCD-

Let there be a golden shine
that lights the sand dunes grassy vine
Bent and tattered
beneath the blue
Holding on to all things true
Lost horizon's ego swells
washing along where dreamers dwell
Incoming tides are echoes of friends
providing life's sound
the dancing begins
Gracefully the sea oats
start to sway
As tomorrow awaits and
today fades away

2/18/13

SHINE

Inspiration from an empty
bottle of yesterday!
Getting lost may be
the path to everywhere
Human nature finds peace
within all boundaries
Roaming along the shores
of runaway tides
Under a blue sky beyond
an exploding horizon
Come absorb life
as the day chases
the sun

2/8/13

94

I await the smile of a particular flower
A solo bouquet scattered across an
empty field — I watch patiently with
Eyes wide open — She stumbles near
me as I stagger closer — I want
to touch her but find her beauty
too fragile — This interuption
in life turns darkness into light
Never needing the acceptance
of any true horizon — Sunrises
and sunsets — Everything else
in between is only noise — Delight
me silently with the warmth
of all kindness — Melt into
my heart the flower
of my dreams — ◁CD—

8/21/14

Rotation of endless nights
and restless days off May
Poetry on the house
Your drinks you have to pay
Empty thoughts Empty bottles
empty pockets to set fire
Wasted breaths and charcoal
collecting one last memory
Reflections of yesterday
neon on the rocks
Invasion of happiness
hate never knocks
Crowded are the voices
we keep out of violence
Ente through here LIFE's
revolving door of silence

96

Distract me with your kindness
Subtle winds from afar ——
Allow my thoughts to echoe softly
beyond these four walls ——
I have seen a wilted flower
blossom in the dark ——
She blooms still quietly
with tears in her heart ——
Every day is yesterday if you
avoid the storms of tomorrow ——
Waiting for it to rain ——
Patiently waiting for the rain

9/8/14

Our faces of sadness
   eyes full of tears
Why is it happiness
   is our deepest fears
We walk into our vague
   memories that stand still
Reaching for comfort
   as we breathe and feel
When the smoke clears
   and we see ourselves smile
That is when we realize
   tomorrow is worthwhile

Johnny   11/28/13

Surprise me after
an afternoon rain
Puddle of thoughts
from yesterday remain
Rainbows appear when
your head is in the clouds
Daydreams of wonder
when you dream aloud
Wake me up when
she notices my smile
Flowers in her hair
nature in style
I await everything
that catches me by surprise
I anticipate the smile
in her eyes

Take from us the freedoms for which we have taken for granted — Grant us all another gust of wind to assist us on our journeys — Provide us maps of our souls so that we can follow our hearts — Give us courage to retreat if we are heading in the wrong directions — Getting lost is necessary if we want to find the right path — Escaping yesterday to find a new day the same as it was — May time cast shadows upon us so we can continue chasing the sun —

ohnn

8/4/14

Emptiness is a hug
  with no memorable embrace
Wander with your heart
  across a journey of dreams
Holding on tightly to a past
  we wish to replace
Each day a destination
  farther than it seems
Letting go of a light
  that keeps us in the dark
Perception of time the gaze
  of a melting sun
We search for escape
  these lost days we embark
Waking up to the glory that
  you are someone
  who is loved than

We Breathe
Because our
Mother's gave us life
We exist because
Mother Nature
allows us to breathe
We are who we are
from love that they
both offer us — Johnny

HAPPY MOTHER'S DAY

Ich Liebe Dich Mutti
Best Bartender of All Time

A Taste of Sunshine

The Clock on the wall says 3 o'clock

Spin the Bottle Night

I find myself
dancing with your shadow
Older than conversation
lost in the wind
Tastes differently with
fresh memories of you
Elapsed thoughts forgotten
in another kiss from yesterday
Ten seconds ahead
taken far away from now
I can smile knowing you
are here without being here

Johnni 10/7/9

Lost in a summer daze
some memories never fade
Far away horizons are
thoughts with no parade
Caressing the sky with
visions from thy soul
Blue reflections that
devour me whole
I admire her smile
beautiful so far away
It shines bright within
me close with each new day

Helpless is a blue sky
  that bleeds into the night
May the journey within your
  heart lead you to higher light
A never ending story and
  a just beginning song
Melody and happiness keeps
  us humming along,
Surrounded by nature's
  canvas these illustrious views
In between the horizons
  of melting days and joyous hues

Johnny

Bring joy to a horizon that hasn't
seen the sun — Create a smile
in a stranger's heart today —
Balance your soul befor the
ice begins to melt — A toast
toward the heavens once your tears
find a friend — Memories of
yesterday always return home
Surrounded by loved ones that wander
through these doors — We are
strangers only to ourselves if we
forget how to smile — Smile
and I will smile too — If this
were a mirror you would be
smiling at you . . . . . .

Johnny 7/14/15

110

I SEEM TO ALWAYS
LEAVE HERE EARLY MORNING
IN MY SLEEP THE NEON
LIGHTS ARE STILL BURNING
WHEN THE SMOKE CLEARS
AND THE SPIRIT CHASES
I FIND MYSELF IN
FAR AWAY PLACES
WAKE ME WHEN YOU
FIND ME ALONE
ALL BY MYSELF ON
MY WAY HOME

I have escaped life's
    shadow without saying a word
Wandering in silence   my thoughts
    roam unheard — The echoe
of my heartbeat travels with the wind
Creating a circle of love
    and amazing friends
An abundance of warmth
    I will never go cold
A new sun rises
    I will never feel old

2/16/16

I AM A VOICE
IN A FAR AWAY FOREST
..MY. D.I.S.G.U.I.S.E echoes
Beyond the richest of the poorest
I AM THE SHADE IN THE
MIDDLE of the day
A falling leaf that
finds it's way
Winding through a
stream of the unknown
Enjoying life's reflection
of happiness fully grown
5/3/14

Wander through the fog
of an early morning smoke
Rise beyond the silence
the radiant light revokes
Shine quietly amidst your fears
and far away dreams
Awaken to the rush of life's
never ending stream
Stagger through the
noise of a far
away quest
Discover a joy
you will find
ubiquitous   5/10/16

Shine down upon this landscape
  of a lost mankind
My heart wanders quietly
   through a far away forest
It follows life's trail that fades
   into the sky — An elevated
horizon the grandest view of all
Visible through the clouds are
falling tears for rising souls

Nurturing seeds of hope
  so PEACE and
LOVE can
Blossom — 6-12-16

JCD

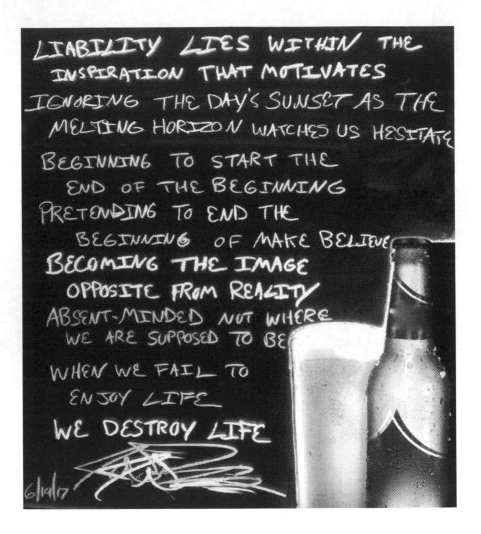

LIABILITY LIES WITHIN THE
INSPIRATION THAT MOTIVATES
IGNORING THE DAY'S SUNSET AS THE
MELTING HORIZON WATCHES US HESITATE
BEGINNING TO START THE
END OF THE BEGINNING
PRETENDING TO END THE
BEGINNING OF MAKE BELIEVE
BECOMING THE IMAGE
OPPOSITE FROM REALITY
ABSENT-MINDED NOT WHERE
WE ARE SUPPOSED TO BE
WHEN WE FAIL TO
ENJOY LIFE
WE DESTROY LIFE

6/14/17

Sunset Wishes

Full Bar Service

Beetle Gin and Juice

Magical Merlin
- Lenny -

Waiting in silence for the
noise to appear from a darkness
that awaits the days fresh breath of air
Awakened by a breeze that hurries along
beyond todays horizon fresh in song

Dreaming in color as the early sun
rises, spreading joy through
natures disguises
Enjoying freedom
and our journey
of souls along life's
trail of heavenly
strolls

8/15/16

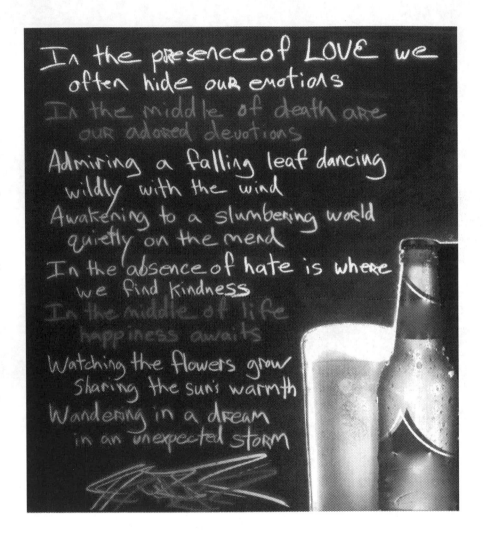

In the presence of LOVE we
often hide our emotions
In the middle of death are
our adored devotions
Admiring a falling leaf dancing
wildly with the wind
Awakening to a slumbering world
quietly on the mend
In the absence of hate is where
we find kindness
In the middle of life
happiness awaits
Watching the flowers grow
Sharing the suns warmth
Wandering in a dream
in an unexpected storm

FROM THE OUTSIDE PEEKING IN WE ARE
   AN UNKNOWN CIRCLE OF FRIENDS
BROKEN PROMISES STARING
   OUT INTO A DAYDREAM
SIDE BY SIDE WE SIT-A ROOM
   FULL OF BEAUTIFUL STRANGERS
WE ALL WITNESS LIFE STAGGER
   THROUGH THESE TWO DOORS
TARANTISM IS THE SILENT CURE
   TO LIFE'S INDIVIDUAL TEARS
SHARING OUR JOYS THAT
HAVE STRAYED FROM TIME
LET US RAISE OUR
   GLASSES TO THE
SPIRIT OF OUR HEARTS

8/14/17

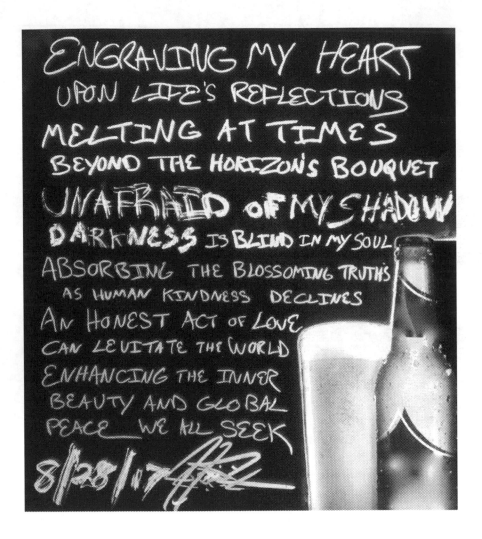

ENGRAVING MY HEART
UPON LIFE'S REFLECTIONS
MELTING AT TIMES
BEYOND THE HORIZON'S BOUQUET
UNAFRAID OF MY SHADOW
DARKNESS IS BLIND IN MY SOUL
ABSORBING THE BLOSSOMING TRUTHS
AS HUMAN KINDNESS DECLINES
AN HONEST ACT OF LOVE
CAN LEVITATE THE WORLD
ENHANCING THE INNER
BEAUTY AND GLOBAL
PEACE WE ALL SEEK
8/28/07

A LOST BREATH IN AN UNCONTROLLED
GUST OF WIND — I FIND MYSELF
STARING INTO THE ABYSS OF AN UNKNOWN
ENTITY — AWAKEN ME FROM THE
EXPERIENCES I HAVE YET TO AWAKEN TO
— A RECENT SMILE HAS BROUGHT ME
TO A SMILE — THE WEIGHT OF TRUTH
UPON A FALSE FRONT SHARES CLARITY
— I FEARED THAT THE SEA OATS
WOULD DROWN WITH THE TIDES
— YESTERDAY WAS TODAY
BUT IN A DIFFERENT STATE
OF MIND — I AM LIVING
IN SPIRIT AND DYING
IN BODY — IT IS SO
BEAUTIFUL OUT HERE ON
THIS MELTING HORIZON
— I CAN'T FIND IT IN
MY HEART TO GO BACK INSIDE

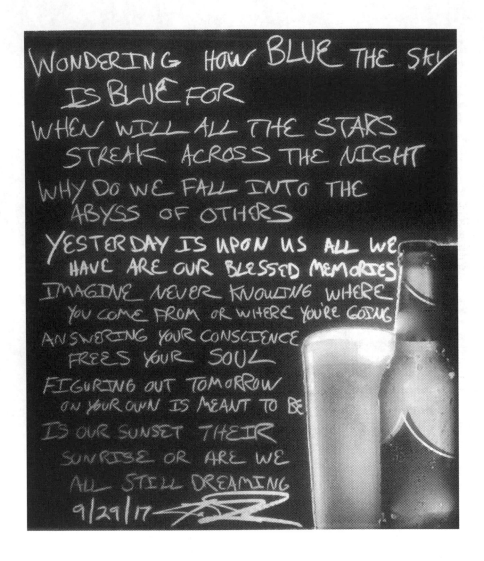

WONDERING HOW BLUE THE SKY
IS BLUE FOR
WHEN WILL ALL THE STARS
STREAK ACROSS THE NIGHT
WHY DO WE FALL INTO THE
ABYSS OF OTHERS
YESTERDAY IS UPON US ALL WE
HAVE ARE OUR BLESSED MEMORIES
IMAGINE NEVER KNOWING WHERE
YOU COME FROM OR WHERE YOU'RE GOING
ANSWERING YOUR CONSCIENCE
FREES YOUR SOUL
FIGURING OUT TOMORROW
ON YOUR OWN IS MEANT TO BE
IS OUR SUNSET THEIR
SUNRISE OR ARE WE
ALL STILL DREAMING
9/29/17

REMEMBER TO BREATHE
WITH EVERY MOMENT LIVED
UPON THE HORIZON OF TODAY
CAPTURE A MEMORY
FADE INTO THE DISTANCE
FOOTPRINTS AND MELODIES
WILDLY WITHIN YOUR HEART
AN ECHO CAN DANCE
WITH EVERY MOMENT LIVED
REMEMBER TO BREATHE
CAPTURE A MEMORY UPON
THE HORIZON OF TODAY
FOOTPRINTS AND MELODIES
FADE INTO THE DISTANCE
AN ECHO CAN DANCE
WILDLY WITIN
YOUR HEART
11/13/17

FINDING OUT YOU ARE OUT OF CONTROL
WANDER IN SPIRIT YOU BEAUTIFUL SOUL
WHEN LIFE'S TRAIL AT TIMES SEEMS DARK AND COLD
ANOTHER CHAPTER OF A STORY UNTOLD
DANCE UPON A HORIZON EASY TO FIND
STRAY IN THOUGHT NOT IN MIND
AS THE TIDES WASH YOUR FOOTPRINTS AWAY
TURN THE PAGE OF ANOTHER DAY
LOST PROMISES A WALK BECOMES A RUN
SO YOUR HEARTBEAT CAN CHASE THE SUN
FORGIVING WHY WE SHOULD NEVER CRY
A NEW RAIN HAS REMINDED US WHY
OMINOUS CLOUDS AND BLUE SKY MYSTERIES
DAYDREAMS BECOME INSTANT
MEMORIES
COMPREHEND WHERE YOU
HAVE BEEN
THE SUN WILL SLOWLY
ESCAPE AGAIN

11/27/17

A thought that becomes
a journey on canvas / I hunger
for a walk into an unknown
forest Paint for me a dream
my soul inspires to chase
Create illustrious skies
of blue emitting
heavens grace
Light the trail
from above to guide
me along each day
Loving me with the
mystery of Mother
Nature every breath
of the wind

The sun radiates bright with purpose
this day as a young soul has ascended
beyond our horizon — Azure rays of light
comforts our hearts as we drown in sadness
Joy from heaven above echoes triumphantly
the love of a wonderful man — Every new
gust within the winds will emit truth
of his flight exceeding all the stars.
Forever shining down upon us every
evening until the early mornings
shine — His smile reminds
us that time can stand still
Lost in his Memory for now
found in his kindness —
Comforting us through the noise
of life created by silence
Share with us now the journey
of living As we await your
reflection in our river of dreams
OUR ETERNAL BROTHER —MikeWolf

The Sun is Over the Yardarm

Scottish Birthday Kiss

Johnny Sandwich Karen Style

AMEN

Underage Happy Hour

TRUE CHARACTER COMES
FROM WALKING THE SAME
PATH SO MANY OTHERS HAVE
WALKED BEFORE, WITHOUT LOS[
YOUR IDENTITY.

IT IS DEFINED BY THE
SELFLESS ACTS WE COMMIT,
AND IT SHINES THROUGH THE
COMPASSION WE SHOW TO
OTHERS.

Steve Clarke

Hi - I'm Batman

Johnny and Twitch
- Shine for Me -

Getting Keys to the Cadillac

Seven Year Itch
- Appalachian Trail Here I Come -

I staggered into the quiet of darkness to have a conversation with an old friend -

The age of yesterday spoke back to me through the silence of time -

I was told that fewer are climbing the mountains for a better view of their lives -

While others hide in the light running away from themselves -

i was asked if I was afraid of the dark -

I replied with a bright smile gone unnoticed -

I stared into the blackness of the night noticed the eyes of my own shadow -

At first sight I discovered it was the reflection of my soul -

Afraid of the dark you ask -

I am only afraid of myself -

-JCD-

The past of all tomorrow's will soon find its way -

You shine in my heart like the light of a new day -

We are always together in my photographic mind -

Melting in memory your sunset still I find -

Silence surrounds me often when I think of you -

Expression in repetition the horizon's transmuted view -

It whispers a warmth only the sun can hear -

It is always your loving smile that keeps you so near -

-JCD-

In Loving Memory of My Mother
- Elizabeth M. DeRosa -

Made You Look

Buzz and Vern
- Champion of Kindness -

Printed in the United States
By Bookmasters